BOULDER CITY LIBRARY

3 1432 00180 0588

D0778557

J   Orr, Nicole
BIO
RIDLEY   Daisy Ridley

BOULDER CITY LIBRARY
701 ADAMS BLVD.
BOULDER CITY, NV 89005

DISCARD

A BEACON • BIOGRAPHY

Daisy Ridley

Nicole K. Orr

PURPLE TOAD
PUBLISHING

DISCARD

BOULDER CITY LIBRARY
701 ADAMS BLVD.
BOULDER CITY, NV 89005

AUG   2017

PURPLE TOAD
PUBLISHING

Copyright © 2017 by Purple Toad Publishing, Inc. All rights reserved. No part of this book may be reproduced without written permission from the publisher. Printed and bound in the United States of America.

Printing   1   2   3   4   5   6   7   8   9

A Beacon Biography

Angelina Jolie
Big Time Rush
Cam Newton
Carly Rae Jepsen
Daisy Ridley
Drake
Ed Sheeran
Ellen DeGeneres
Elon Musk
Harry Styles of One Direction
Jennifer Lawrence
John Boyega
Kevin Durant
Lorde
Malala
Maria von Trapp
Markus "Notch" Persson, Creator of Minecraft
Mo'ne Davis
Muhammad Ali
Neil deGrasse Tyson
Peyton Manning
Robert Griffin III (RG3)

Publisher's Cataloging-in-Publication Data
Orr, Nicole.
   Daisy Ridley / written by Nicole Orr.
      p. cm.
Includes bibliographic references, glossary, and index.
ISBN 9781624692604
1. Ridley, Daisy, 1992- —Juvenile literature. 2. Motion picture actors and actresses—Great Britain—Biography—Juvenile literature. I. Series: Beacon biography.
 PN2598 2017
 791.43
                                             Library of Congress Control Number: 2016936309

eBook ISBN: 9781624692611

ABOUT THE AUTHOR: Nicole K. Orr has been writing for as long as she's known how to hold a pen. She is the author of two other titles by Purple Toad Publishing and has won National Novel Writing Month nine times. Orr lives in Portland, Oregon, and camps under the stars whenever she can. When she isn't writing, she's taking road trips or jetting around the world. What would she do with the Force if she had it? She'd mind-control airport security to let her fly anywhere she wanted to, for free!

PUBLISHER'S NOTE: This story has not been authorized or endorsed by Daisy Ridley.

CONTENTS

*British actress Daisy Ridley knew she might have to travel for the new **Star Wars** movie. What she didn't know was that she'd end up in the middle of nowhere.*

Dangers Unseen

It's a hot day in Rub' al Khali (*roob al HAH-lee*), the desert of Abu Dhabi, United Arab Emirates. There isn't a cloud in the sky. The sun is burning overhead. Not a single breeze disturbs the dunes. In every direction, there is nothing to see but a wasteland so alien, it could be another planet.

Rub' al Khali, the Empty Quarter, is as red as Mars and as dusty as the Old West. With almost no rain from year to year, very little grows here. There are no rivers, lakes, or oceans. There is no grass, and there are no trees. There is, however, a Daisy.

Daisy Ridley lies on her back on the sand. Her hair is tied up high on her head and sweat is running down the sides of her face. From shoulder to foot, she wears mummy-like wrappings. She's been lying here for hours. Above her, actors, cameramen, and directors hustle about, filming a scene.

In the Empty Quarter, most of the dangers are clear. There's the burning sunshine. There's the hot sand. There's the desert itself, menacing in its lack of water or shade. However, there are also dangers that are harder to see. There is a deadly scorpion. Its sting requires medical treatment within half an hour or its victim will die. Ridley knows that she and the rest of the crew are more than an hour from a hospital. She keeps an eye out for little legs in the sand, imagining the stab of a scorpion's tail. She looks and she worries, but she does not move until the scene is done.[1]

The fat-tailed scorpion is one of the many species of scorpion that calls Rub' al Khali home. Another name for this scorpion is the deathstalker. It takes great bravery to be anywhere near this creature.

A war between good and evil. A fight between planets and ways of life. A fight involving cultures from different planets. A battle between light and dark. These are the star wars that give the series its name. There are many sides in this ongoing siege. There are the Jedi and the Sith. They both wield a supernatural power that is as good or evil as its user. There are also the Rebels. These are people who have no power themselves, but fight for what they believe is right. Innocents get drawn into the chaos. One of these innocents is a desert scavenger named Rey. In *Star Wars: The Force Awakens*, Rey is drawn into the plot against her will. She is lucky she is not alone. A robot named BB-8 follows her around like a puppy. Her friend Finn gets dragged from one disaster to the next right along with her. And there are Han Solo and Chewbacca. One is a smuggler, played by Harrison Ford, and the other is a furry creature called a Wookie. Both help Rey and Finn to survive.

Rey may not have wanted to join this ongoing war, but Daisy Ridley did. A determined young woman, she was the perfect actor to play the role.

One day, Ridley was asked what she would do if she had the Force in real life. She talked about busy days in London, England when she would take an escalator down to the Tube, or subway. It frustrated her when the crowd would not follow common courtesy. People who are not in a hurry should stand on the left side. This allows people who are in a hurry to pass on the right. (This is the opposite of how it's done in the United States.) When slower people stand on the wrong side, they create traffic jams. If she had the Force, Ridley said, she would use it to move people to the correct side of the escalator![2]

An escalator takes people down to the Tube and up to street level in London, England.

London's West End is a popular area to see plays or operas.

In Black Widow's Shoes

In West London, England's young Daisy Jazz Isobel Ridley sat in front of the television. She was grinning from ear to ear. Her eyes were fastened to the TV screen. She had seen the movie *Matilda* dozens of times, and it always left her in awe. What kid wouldn't envy Matilda? Even though she was unhappy in her strict school, and she often felt out of place at home, she had magical powers. Ridley watched and felt a strange feeling in her stomach. What was that? It just might have been inspiration.

Daisy Ridley grew up with creative role models. Her father, Chris Ridley, was a photographer. Her mother, Louise-Corbett Fawkner, worked for a bank. Ridley had two sisters. Poppy-Sophia was a musician. Kika-Rose had been a model since she was ten years old. From 1968 to 1977, Ridley's great-uncle Arnold Ridley played a private eye in the British TV comedy *Dad's Army*.

It isn't clear just when the first spark for acting struck Daisy. According to an interview with *The Guardian*, she didn't have an "ah-ha" moment. "My sister asked me, 'Why do people want to be actors?' I had no answer," she admitted.[1]

The Tring Park School of the Performing Arts was where Ridley felt her first real sense of belonging.

Like most children, Daisy had a lot of dreams. She also had help in following those dreams. When she enrolled at the Tring Park School of the Performing Arts in London, England, her father was one of the first to recognize her talents. He saw her acting and singing abilities and he knew she had a future in those areas. Her mother was the one who found the performing arts school and enrolled her daughter there. The school is featured in the 2015 movie *Avengers: Age of Ultron.* In the movie, the character Black Widow flashes back to her training in a ballet school.[2] Did Ridley's mother sense the school's future stardom? Maybe not, but it is fun to imagine the Avengers' Black Widow and Star Wars' Rey dancing on the same floors.

Going to school at Tring Park awakened a love of singing in Ridley before it did acting. Two of her best talents are singing jazz and cabaret songs. She also learned how to dance and play the violin. She began dreaming not of the big screen, but of musicals, starring in big productions, such as *Wicked* or *Chicago*.

At Tring Park, she was enjoying the arts. She wasn't seriously looking to the future just yet, but the future might have been looking at her.

While at Tring Park, Ridley began to imagine her future. As she fell in love with musicals, such as **Wicked**, *she realized her dreams were getting bigger.*

Daisy Ridley's journey began with elf hats and sparkles, as with this young girl. She then transformed into an actress able to use CPR to save a life—or at least pretend to.

From Christmas Elf to *Star Wars*

Did Ridley's life as an actress begin with a big movie title or a flashy theater performance? No. Before melting in the Rub' al Khali desert, she was wearing pointy shoes and a hat. Long before the Force, she was spreading Santa's cheerful magic. Ridley's acting career started as a Christmas elf at a shopping mall. After she played the elf, she was promoted to princess.

There were other simple roles, too. She was in a music video called "Lights On" by rapper Wiley. She was also in a short film called *Crossed Wires*. She even appeared in an app created for tablets and cell phones. Called *Lifesaver*, the app used different scenes to teach people how to perform CPR (cardiopulmonary resuscitation). In one scene, Ridley plays a woman who finds a man who has fallen in a parking garage. She helps him by giving him CPR.

When interviewed later, Ridley admitted why the project was so important to her. Her grandfather had had a heart attack. His life was saved when someone gave him CPR. *Lifesaver* was nominated for a British Academy of Film and Television Arts Award.[1]

Blue Season was a spooky film made in 2013. In it, Ridley plays a kidnapping victim. The film was part of the SCI-FI-LONDON 48 hour Film Challenge. Teams were given two days to write and shoot a short film. Georgina Higgins was the producer and scriptwriter. In an interview with

The Guardian, Higgins shared her thoughts on Ridley. "She was focused and giving, and open, asking if there was anything she should change or do. We didn't have much time for rehearsals and she worked really well with that. For the first part of the film, she was mostly hanging upside down."[2]

Ridley got quite a few parts in TV shows, too. She was on *Mr. Selfridge, Youngers, Casualty, Toast of London*, and the BBC TV show *Silent Witness*.

In 2015, Ridley was in the film *Scrawl*. Peter Hearn of Andover College wrote and directed the project. The film was about a comic book artist whose creations become real. Ridley played Hannah, one of those creations. "There was something about her. She just had that spark about her," Hearn told *The Guardian*.[3]

In a smile or a sob, Ridley could capture a character in one look—as she does here in **Scrawl**.

Ridley almost had a role in the full-length film *Inbetweeners 2*. Her part was removed at the last minute. Co-creator Iain Morris said that this had nothing to do with Ridley. "We've cut her out of the film," he explained to *Digital Spy*. "She [was] in the opening of the film. We reshot the opening because the script didn't work. We desperately wanted Daisy to come back and do it because she's brilliant, really funny. But by that point she was doing *Star Wars*."[4]

Ridley's life was definitely becoming a roller coaster. The next stop on the ride would be an audition for a new *Star Wars* movie. Fast-forward through three more auditions, and Ridley would be waiting for a phone call from the director of *Star Wars* himself, J.J. Abrams.

As Ridley grew more popular all over the world, so did her sense of fashion. People wanted to know about her likes and dislikes as much as they wanted to dress like her.

edy

COMIC-CON J.J. Abrams
INTERNATIONAL

DIEGO
MIC

Director J.J. Abrams (left) sits with Lawrence Kasdan, co-writer of The Force Awakens, at the 2015 San Diego Comic-Con. Abrams is about to introduce Daisy Ridley to the fans attending the convention and, thanks to countless cameras, to the rest of the fans around the world.

Becoming Rey

Ridley stood on the sidewalk in London, England. The sounds of a busy city surrounded her. Carefully, she returned one of the most important phone calls of her life. She went completely still when the call finally went through. She heard the voice of J.J. Abrams on the other end.

The call didn't last long. Minutes after she hung up, Ridley rode the subway home. Only she knew that she had just been granted a role in the new *Stars Wars* movie. She had promised not to talk about it.[1]

Ridley went through more than four auditions for *Star Wars* before she got the role. She doubted herself every step of the way. However, Abrams liked her from the beginning. "When you walked past her in the waiting room, she was just sort of alight," he told *The Inquisitr*.[2]

Once Ridley got the role, she became nervous. "I didn't celebrate," she explained in a conversation with *Refinery29*. "I thought I was going to lose the part the whole time. Honestly, I was like, they've made a terrible mistake. I went for brunch the next day with my agents, and they were celebrating. I just felt sick and, like, I didn't want to be there. It's just so much to process."[3] Was she at least a bit excited? "It took a long time for it to settle in," she told *The Daily Mail*. "I thought I was in *The Twilight Zone*."[4]

Ridley and her *Star Wars* costar, John Boyega, got along even better in real life than their characters did in the movie. The two had a lot in common.

John Boyega and Daisy Ridley were both very new to the big screen. The friendship they formed gave them confidence.

They were both 23 years old. Both had been born in London, England. When *Star Wars* began filming in Abu Dhabi, United Arab Emirates, the two took walks through the city markets. They sang songs from the movie *The Lion King.* Some fans believed the actors were a couple. When speaking with *Entertainment Weekly,* Ridley explained she and Boyega are "like brother and sister. . . . We get on really well and we make each other laugh. Sadly, people think a guy and girl can't be friends without something romantic going on."[5]

Ridley was quite nervous when filming began. In fact, Abrams told Ridley her performance was "wooden." "This was the first day!" Ridley said in an interview with *Cinema Blend.* "And I honestly wanted to die. I thought I was gonna cry, I couldn't breathe."[6]

However, Abrams was actually one of Ridley's biggest fans. "Daisy is so tough, while also able to reveal how human she is," he said in an interview

One of the challenges to filming in the desert was the constant dust.

with *Ace of Geeks.* "There was one day on set when some sparks went off around her, and one went down her back and burned her a little. It was more scary than it was physically painful, but she took a minute, shook it off, and we were back up and running in 15 minutes."[7] Ridley grew more comfortable as time passed. When *Elle* later asked her to describe Abrams, Ridley said simply, "He's a massive nerd!"[8]

To get into shape to play Rey, Ridley ate carefully and exercised daily. She trained for three months, five days a week, five hours a day. She learned the *bojutsu* fighting style. This style involves

using a staff weapon. Kathleen Kennedy, the president of Lucasfilm, told *The International Business Times*, "Daisy's gotten to be so good at *bojutsu* that even grown men on the set fear it."[9]

Lucasfilm chief and architect of the new movie, Kathleen Kennedy

As good as Ridley was with a staff, the directors still hired Chloe Bruce as a stunt double. Bruce is a world champion martial artist. She began training in martial arts when she was eight years old. In 2010, she set a Guinness World Record for doing 212 kicks in one minute. Before *Star Wars*, she was a stunt double in the movies *Guardians of the Galaxy* and *Thor: The Dark World*.[10]

Did Ridley find it scary to work with big names like Harrison Ford and Carrie Fisher, who plays Princess Leia? Definitely! The first time she and Ford walked into the *Millennium Falcon* cockpit, Ridley stole the pilot's chair from Han Solo himself! Ford laughed. Then, he gave her some piloting advice.[11]

Ridley told *Entertainment Weekly*, "I was doing random switch-flipping, but I was probably flipping switches a bit too much, and Harrison kind of put his hand out and said, no, everything had to have a purpose. Like, you flip a switch and then you see what it does, before you do anything else. I was probably flipping switches too quickly!"[12]

Star Wars: The Force Awakens *brought together the franchise's original stars. From left to right, Carrie Fisher, Mark Hamill, and Harrison Ford.*

Carrie Fisher spent much of her time in 1983's **Return of the Jedi** *chained to a throne. Here, she gets a chance to escape for some ocean fun!*

Carrie Fisher made Ridley laugh. Once, Fisher joked that she and Ridley should go to Las Vegas, Nevada, dressed in their *Star Wars* costumes. Another time, Fisher pointed out a *Star Wars* shop next to a McDonald's. She called it "McStar Wars." The two actors had similar senses of humor. Fisher also helped Ridley settle into a new generation of *Star Wars* women— ones that don't wear metal bikinis as Princess Leia once did.

In 2015, Ridley was part of a contest hosted by J.J. Abrams. Fans were invited to give $10 to one of the charities chosen by the cast of *Star Wars: The Force Awakens.* Winners would be invited to see a special showing of the movie in London, England, or Los Angeles. Ridley chose a charity on public health.[13]

Ridley might have hoped to relax once the film was released. However, the Rey action figures, the people wearing Rey costumes, and the fan conventions would keep her busy.

Daisy Ridley and John Boyega at an event to launch their Disney Infinity action figure likenesses and the Star Wars: The Force Awakens *videogame.*

Childhood Heroes

Long before the *Star Wars* movie was released, Ridley attended a fan convention. She posted on Twitter, "Five thousand people screaming your name, and they don't know who you are or what part you play, they just know you're part of something they love—that's special."[1] Fan conventions are just one way Ridley has stayed busy since the movie finished filming. What else has she been up to? According to *Tumblr*, she's been baking BB-8 cakes. She has shared her recipe with the world and inspired many YouTube videos.

In October 2015, Ridley and BB-8 appeared on an English postage stamp.[2] They are shown in the desert on the planet Jakku. Ridley has also stayed in touch with Oscar Isaac. He is the actor who plays risky pilot Poe Dameron in the movie. Isaac and Ridley are both singers. They posted an online video of them singing "Baby, It's Cold Outside" together.

Ridley also uses her free time to watch TV, while snuggling her deaf and blind dog, Muffin. *House of Cards* and *RuPaul's Drag Race* are two of her favorite shows. She has also been making up for what she missed out on as a kid. She is watching all the *Star Wars* movies! When talking with *Elle*, Ridley admitted she "sort of missed the whole *Star Wars* thing—and I don't think it's because I'm a girl. It's just that no one in my immediate family was a big fan."[3]

Ridley also spends time with another actor, long-time boyfriend Charlie Hamblett. He has performed in a number of plays, as well as in the TV miniseries *Babylon*. Hamblett calls Ridley "my beautiful nerd." In 2015, the couple was seen cuddling at a Halloween party, dressed as zombies.[4]

The next *Star Wars* movie wasn't scheduled to be released until 2017, but fans could see more of Ridley in other projects. One is a movie called *Only Yesterday*. The film first came out in Japan more than 25 years ago, but it was rerecorded with English dubbing. Ridley provides the voice for Taeko, a young woman leaving home for the first time. She is going on a journey to find out who she is. Ridley told *Entertainment Weekly*, "I think the reason probably this is such a loved film and will continue to be so is because it doesn't feel foreign. It feels exactly right, like, how do you make your dreams come true?"[5]

Only Yesterday *is an animated film by Studio Ghibli, the same studio that* produced Spirited Away *and* Princess Mononoke.

The movie* The Eagle Huntress *is Ridley's first experience producing instead of acting.

In 2016, Ridley was the producer of a documentary. *The Eagle Huntress* is a story about 13-year-old Aisholpan. Her dream is to become the first female eagle hunter. In an interview with *Deadline Hollywood*, Ridley said, "I was deeply moved by Aisholpan's story and wanted to be a part of this beautiful film. I feel audiences and young girls around the world will be as inspired by her story as I was, and I am so proud to share her journey with the world."[6]

Ridley also talked with *The Hollywood Reporter* about enrolling in college. She is interested in a degree in social science. "I always felt interested in it. People really benefit from talking about what's going on, and the people who help others get through awful points in their life are actually amazing. To touch someone who's going through something would be very fulfilling. Then again, I get very emotional so I don't know whether I would get too involved in things."[7]

All over the world, at Comic Cons and movie releases, fans are dressing up as Ridley's character, Rey.

Mara Wilson, as she appeared in Matilda *(1996), and in 2015*

In 2015, Ridley won the Breakout Award from Florida Film Critics. The next year, she received another award at the Oscar Wilde Award Ceremony. This event honors individuals who are Irish. Ridley is part Irish.

Ridley has come out of her *Star Wars* experience with more confidence. She certainly has more job choices available to her than before. Still, there's not much that can beat talking to a childhood hero.

Mara Wilson played the main character in the movie *Matilda*. She heard about how many times Ridley had watched that movie. According to *Mashable*, Wilson went on Ridley's Twitter page to say, "I was SUCH a *Star Wars* fan as a kid, I used to dream of being in a *Star Wars* movie. But inspiring someone is even better!"

Daisy came back with the simple message: "Life. Made."[8]

For all Ridley knows, she may just be the inspiration for countless other little Reys.

1992	Daisy Ridley is born on April 10 in Westminster, London, England.
2001	Ridley enrolls in the Tring Park School for the Performing Arts in Hertfordshire, England.
2010	Ridley performs in a school production of *The Boyfriend*. She graduates from the Tring Park School for Performing Arts. She enrolls at Birkbeck, University of London, then drops out.
2013	Ridley participates in creating an app called *Lifesaver*.
2014	Ridley auditions for *Star Wars: Episode VII—The Force Awakens*.
2015	Ridley is featured on a *Star Wars* postage stamp issued by the UK Royal Mail Postage Service. She receives the Breakout Award from Florida Film Critics and a Twitter message from childhood hero Mara Wilson.
2016	Ridley receives the Oscar Wilde Award. She begins filming *Star Wars: Episode VIII*.

FILMOGRAPHY

2016 *Only Yesterday* (Voice)

2015 *Disney Infinity 3.0* (Video Game)

Scrawl (Movie)

Star Wars: Episode VII: The Force Awakens (Movie)

2014 *Silent Witness* (TV Series)

Mr. Selfridge (TV Series)

2013 *Lifesaver* (App)

Casualty (TV Series)

Blue Season (Short film)

Youngers (TV Series)

Toast of London (TV Series)

100% Beef (Short film)

Crossed Wires (Short film)

"Lights On" (Music video with Wiley)

PHOTO CREDITS: Cover, pp. 16, 19, 20, 22, 26—Gage Skidmore; pp. 1, 22—Disney/ABC Television; pp. 6, 8, 21—Public Domain; p. 11—Imagine Communications; p. 12—Kryziz Bonny; p. 19—Love4Glamour; p. 24—Amal FM; p. 26—Tomasz Stasiuk; All other photos—cc-by-sa-2.0. Every measure has been taken to find all copyright holders of material used in this book. In the event any mistakes or omissions have happened within, attempts to correct them will be made in future editions of the book.

Chapter One. Dangers Unseen

1. Lorraine Ali, "The Harsh Reality of Building a 'Star Wars' Fantasy in Abu Dhabi," *Los Angeles Times*, December 3, 2015.

2. Olivia Lidbury, "Who's That Girl: 'Star Wars' Actress Daisy Ridley," *The Telegraph*, November 27, 2015.

Chapter Two. In Black Widow's Shoes

1. Emine Saner, "How Daisy Ridley Went from Bit Parts to Lead in 'Star Wars: The Force Awakens,' " *The Guardian*, November 28, 2015.

2. Benjamin Hart, "Daisy Ridley Talks 'The Force Awakens' with EW." *Star Wars Underworld*. April 25, 2015.

Chapter Three. From Christmas Elf to *Star Wars*

1. "Friends of the RC. (UK) Daisy Ridley-Actress." *Resuscitation Council*. UK.

2. Emine Saner, "How Daisy Ridley Went from Bit Parts to Lead in 'Star Wars: The Force Awakens,' " *The Guardian*, November 28, 2015.

3. Ibid.

4. Ben Falk, " 'Star Wars: Episode VII' Star Daisy Ridley Cut Out of 'Inbetweeners 2,' " *Digital Spy*, August 1, 2014.

Chapter Four. Becoming Rey

1. Baz Bamigboye. "Daisy's a Force for the Future—Polite, Genuinely Curious, with a Ready Laugh," *Daily Mail*, December 3, 2015.

2. Ernie Howell, "Daisy Ridley Launches Her Career with 'Star Wars: The Force Awakens.' " *The Inquisitr*, December 6, 2015.

3. Missy Schwartz, "Daisy Ridley Tells Us What It's Like to Hug Chewbacca," *Refinery29*, December 4, 2015.

4. Bamigboye.

5. Anthony Breznican, "Daisy Ridley & John Boyega are Changing 'Star Wars'—and Our World," *Entertainment Weekly*, November 13, 2015.

6. Dirk Libbey, "J.J. Abrams' Surprising Criticism of Daisy Ridley's Early 'Star Wars' Performance," *Cinema Blend*, November, 2015.

7. Melissa Devlin, " 'The Force Awakens' Rey Is a Dream Come True," *Ace of Geeks*, December 19, 2015.

8. Seth Plattner, "Four Reasons Daisy Ridley Is Ready to Be 'Star Wars' First Female Protagonist," *Elle*, November 10, 2015.

9. Tanya Diente, " 'Star Wars: The Force Awakens' Rey's Fighting Style Pays Homage to Darth Maul." *International Business Times*, May 20, 2015.

10. Famous Birthdays, *Chloe Bruce*.

11. Meredith Woerner, "The Women of 'Star Wars: The Force Awakens' Talk about Blasting Barriers," *Portland Press Herald*, December 13, 2015.

12. Breznican.

13. Margaret Lenker, " 'Star Wars' Charity Contest Gives Fans a Chance to Attend 'Force Awakens' Premiere., *Variety Editions*, November 25, 2015.

Chapter Five. Childhood Heroes

1. David Barrett, " 'Star Wars: The Force Awakens' Daisy Ridley Had 'Really Weird Feeling' which Forced Her to Audition," *The Telegraph*, December 13, 2015.

2. Ibid.

3. Seth Plattner, "Can An Unknown Named Daisy Ridley Take Over the 'Star Wars' Empire?" *Elle*, December 18, 2015.

4. Halina Watts and Rod McPhee, "'Star Wars' New Star Daisy Ridley: Dad Praises 'Extraordinary' Daughter After She Lands Episode VII Leading Role," *Mirror*, May 1, 2014.

5. Jeff Labrecque, "Daisy Ridley Gives Voice to Heralded 'Studio Ghibli' Classic, 'Only Yesterday,'" *Entertainment Weekly*, December 28, 2015.

6. Mike Fleming Jr., "'Star Wars' Daisy Ridley Becomes 'Eagle Huntress' Exec Producer—Sundance," *Deadline Hollywood*, January 21, 2016.

7. Tatiana Siegel and Marc Bernardin, "Next Gen 2015: New 'Star Wars' Stars on Anxiety, Rejection, and Sudden Stardom," *The Hollywood Reporter*, November 4, 2015.

8. Melissa Marini, "Daisy Ridley News: How Was 'Star Wars' Star's Life Made By Mara Wilson?" *Mashable*, January 5, 2016.

Books

Fentiman, David. *Star Wars: The Force Awakens: New Adventures*. New York: DK Children, 2015.

Fry, Jason. *"Star Wars: The Force Awakens" Incredible Cross-Sections*. New York: DK Children, 2015.

Kogge, Michael. *"Star Wars: The Force Awakens" Junior Novel*. New York: Disney LucasFilm Press, 2016.

Schaefer, Elizabeth. *"Star Wars: The Force Awakens" Rey's Story*. New York: Disney LucasFilm Press, 2016.

Siglain, Michael. *"Star Wars: The Force Awakens:" Han and Chewie Return!* New York: Disney Lucasfilm Press, 2015.

Szostak, Phil, and LucasFilm Ltd. *The Art of "Star Wars: The Force Awakens."* New York: Abrams Books, 2015.

Works Consulted

Ali, Lorraine. "The Harsh Reality of Building a Star Wars Fantasy in Abu Dhabi." *Los Angeles Times*. December 3, 2015. http://www.latimes.com/entertainment/herocomplex/la-ca-hc-star-wars-filming-abu-dhabi-20151206-story.html

Bamigboye, Baz. "Daisy's a Force for the Future—Polite, Genuinely Curious, with a Ready Laugh." *Daily Mail*. December 3, 2015. http://www.dailymail.co.uk/tvshowbiz/article-3345318/BAZ-BAMIGBOYE-Daisy-s-Force-future-polite-genuinely-curious-ready-laugh.html

Barrett, David. "'Star Wars: The Force Awakens' Daisy Ridley Had "Really Weird Feeling" which Forced Her to Audition." *The Telegraph*. December 13, 2015. http://www.telegraph.co.uk/culture/star-wars/12048080/Star-Wars-The-Force-Awakens-Daisy-Ridley-had-really-weird-feeling-which-forced-her-to-audition.html

Breznican, Anthony. "Daisy Ridley & John Boyega are Changing 'Star Wars'—and Our World." *Entertainment Weekly*. November 13, 2015. http://www.ew.com/article/2015/11/13/daisy-ridley-john-boyega-star-wars-force-awakens

Bugbee, Teo. "Meet Daisy Ridley, Heroine of 'Star Wars: The Force Awakens.' " *The Daily Beast*. December 11, 2015. http://www.thedailybeast.com/articles/2015/12/11/meet-daisy-ridley-heroine-of-star-wars-the-force-awakens.html

Crum, Mandy. "Daisy Ridley Says She Struggled with Seeing Potential in Herself for 'Star Wars' Role." *Inquisitr*. December 27, 2015. http://www.inquisitr.com/2660932/daisy-ridley-says-she-struggled-with-seeing-potential-in-herself-for-star-wars-role/

Devlin, Melissa. "'The Force Awakens' Rey Is a Dream Come True." *Ace of Geeks*. December 19, 2015. http://aceofgeeks.net/11286-2/

Diliberto, Joe. "10 Things You Didn't Know About Daisy Ridley." *National Enquirer*. January 24, 2016. http://www.nationalenquirer.com/celebrity/10-things-you-didnt-know-about-daisy-ridley/

Eames, Tom. "'Star Wars' Episode 7's Daisy Ridley Cut from 'The Inbetweeners 2.'" *Digital Spy*. August 1, 2014. http://www.digitalspy.com/movies/star-wars/news/a587865/star-wars-episode-7s-daisy-ridley-cut-from-the-inbetweeners-2/

Famous Birthdays. *Chloe Bruce*. http://www.famousbirthdays.com/people/chloe-bruce.html

Fleming, Mike, Jr. "'Star Wars' Daisy Ridley Becomes "Eagle Huntress" Exec Producer—Sundance." *Deadline Hollywood*. January 21, 2016. http://deadline.com/2016/01/star-wars-the-force-awakens-daisy-ridley-the-eagle-huntress-sundance-film-festival-1201687900/

Haysom, Sam. "21 Times 'Star Wars' Actress Daisy Ridley's Instagram Was Out of This World Awesome." *Mashable*. January 13, 2016. http://mashable.com/2016/01/13/daisy-ridley-best-instagram-posts/#aXA6JgilAiq9

Howell, Ernie. "Daisy Ridley Launches Her Career with 'Star Wars: The Force Awakens.'" *The Inquisitr*. December 6, 2015. http://www.inquisitr.com/2615852/daisy-ridley-launches-her-career-with-star-wars-the-force-awakens/

Labrecque, Jeff. "Daisy Ridley Gives Voice to Heralded 'Studio Ghibli' Classic, 'Only Yesterday.'" *Entertainment Weekly*. December 28, 2015. http://www.ew.com/article/2015/12/28/daisy-ridley-only-yesterday-exclusive

Lenker, Margaret. "'Star Wars' Charity Contest Gives Fans a Chance to Attend 'Force Awakens' Premiere." *Variety Editions*. November 25, 2015. http://variety.com/2015/film/news/star-wars-premiere-contest-omaze-j-j-abrams-1201648634/

Libbey, Dirk. "J.J. Abrams' Surprising Criticism of Daisy Ridley's Early 'Star Wars' Performance." *Cinema Blend*. November, 2015. http://www.cinemablend.com/new/J-J-Abrams-Surprising-Criticism-Daisy-Ridley-Early-Star-Wars-Performance-97067.html

Lidbury, Olivia. "Who's That Girl: 'Star Wars' Actress Daisy Ridley." *The Telegraph*. November 27, 2015. http://www.telegraph.co.uk/fashion/people/whos-that-girl-star-wars-actress-daisy-ridley/

Lussier, Germain. "Kathleen Kennedy Talks Boba Fett, and Rey's Fighting Style in 'The Force Awakens.'" *SlashFilm*. May 18, 2015. http://www.slashfilm.com/kathleen-kennedy-boba-fett/

Marini, Melissa. "Daisy Ridley News: How Was 'Star Wars' Star's Life Made By Mara Wilson?" *EnStars*. January 5, 2016. http://www.enstarz.com/articles/132607/20160105/daisy-ridley-news-how-was-star-wars-star-s-life-made-by-mara-wilson-photo-video.htm

Oswald, Anjelica. "Here Are the Intense Workouts and Diets the Actors in 'Star Wars: The Force Awakens' Went Through to Prepare for Their Roles." *Business Insider*. December 17, 2015. http://www.businessinsider.com/star-wars-the-force-awakens-actors-workouts-diets-2015-12

Plattner, Seth. "Can An Unknown Named Daisy Ridley Take Over the 'Star Wars' Empire?" *Elle*. December 18, 2015. http://www.elle.com/culture/celebrities/interviews/a31408/daisy-ridley-elle-december-2015-cover-story/

Plattner, Seth. "Four Reasons Daisy Ridley Is Ready to be 'Star Wars' First Female Protagonist." *Elle*. November 10, 2015. http://www.elle.com/culture/movies-tv/news/a31771/daisy-ridley-elle-december/

Saner, Emine. "How Daisy Ridley Went from Bit Parts to Lead in 'Star Wars: The Force Awakens.'" *The Guardian.* November 28, 2015. http://www.theguardian.com/film/2015/nov/28/daisy-ridley-star-wars-the-force-awakens

Schwartz, Missy. "Daisy Ridley Tells Us What It's Like to Hug Chewbacca." *Refinery29.* December 4, 2015. http://www.refinery29.com/2015/12/98808/daisy-ridley-star-wars-force-awakens-interview

Siegel, Tatiana. "Next Gen 2015: How Unknown Daisy Ridley's "Weird Feeling" Helped Her Land 'Star Wars' Role." *The Hollywood Reporter.* November 4, 2015. http://www.hollywoodreporter.com/news/next-gen-2015-how-unknown-836637

Siegel, Tatiana, and Marc Bernardin. "Next Gen 2015: New 'Star Wars' Stars on Anxiety, Rejection, and Sudden Stardom." *The Hollywood Reporter.* November 4, 2015. http://www.hollywoodreporter.com/features/next-gen-2015-new-star-836913

Watts, Halina, and Rod McPhee. "'Star Wars' New Star Daisy Ridley: Dad Praises 'Extraordinary' Daughter After She Lands Episode VII Leading Role." *Mirror.* May 1, 2014. http://www.mirror.co.uk/tv/tv-news/star-wars-vii-daisy-ridley-3481110

Woerner, Meredith. "The Women of 'Star Wars: The Force Awakens' Talks about Blasting Barriers." *Portland Press Herald.* December 13, 2015. http://www.pressherald.com/2015/12/13/the-women-of-star-wars-the-force-awakens-talk-about-blasting-barriers/

On the Internet
"Star Wars: The Force Awakens."
http://www.starwars.com/the-force-awakens/
Star Wars.
http://www.starwars.com/
Star Wars Rey.
http://www.starwars.com/databank/rey

GLOSSARY

Abu Dhabi (ah-boo DAH-bee)—The capital of the United Arab Emirates, a country in the Middle East.

bikini (bih-KEE-nee)—A two-piece swimsuit for women.

bojutsu (boh-JOOT-zoo)—A type of martial art that involves fighting with a "bo" or staff.

cardiopulmonary resuscitation (kar-dee-oh-PUL-muh-nayr-ee ree-sus-ih-TAY-shun)—The lifesaving steps taken to restart the breathing and heartbeat in a person who isn't breathing or whose heart has stopped.

celebrity (seh-LEB-rih-tee)—A famous person.

cockpit (KOK-pit)—The area on an airplane or spaceship where the pilot sits.

documentary (dok-yoo-MEN-tah-ree)—A movie that shows real events.

dub (duhb)—To replace the soundtrack in a movie with one in a different a language, making it seem the actors are speaking the new language.

fan convention (fan kun-VEN-shun)—A formal event that brings together fans with a common interest, such as a movie or TV show.

inspiration (in-spuh-RAY-shun)—A person or event that causes others to want to do something positive.

menacing (MEH-nuh-sing)—Threatening or frightening.

nerd (nurd)—Someone who is very interested in a single subject.

nominate (NAH-mih-nayt)—To suggest a person for an award.

rehearsal (ree-HER-sul)—A practice for a performance.

scriptwriter (SKRIPT-ry-ter)—A person who writes the lines for a movie, play, or other performance.

supernatural (soo-per-NATCH-rul)—Something that seems magical or that is not explained by science.

wasteland (WAYST-land)—A stretch of land with nothing on it.